LITTLE SNAIL

LITTLE SNAIL

Linda Hartley

Photographs by Hidekazu Kubo
GEC Garrett Educational Corporation

The rain comes down.

A tiny snail crawls out.

The little snail climbs a flower stalk.

Long feelers come out of the snail's head.

The black dots at the end of the feelers

are the snail's eyes.

The snail looks around.

It crawls slowly over the plant.

The underside of the leaf

keeps the snail

from getting wet.

Nearby, a butterfly needs a leaf for shelter.

If its wings get wet, it can't fly.

Plop!

What was that?

The little snail sees a tree frog

land on a leaf.

Pling!

The tree frog leaps

from the leaf . . .

far into the air.

The snail is on the move, too, . . .

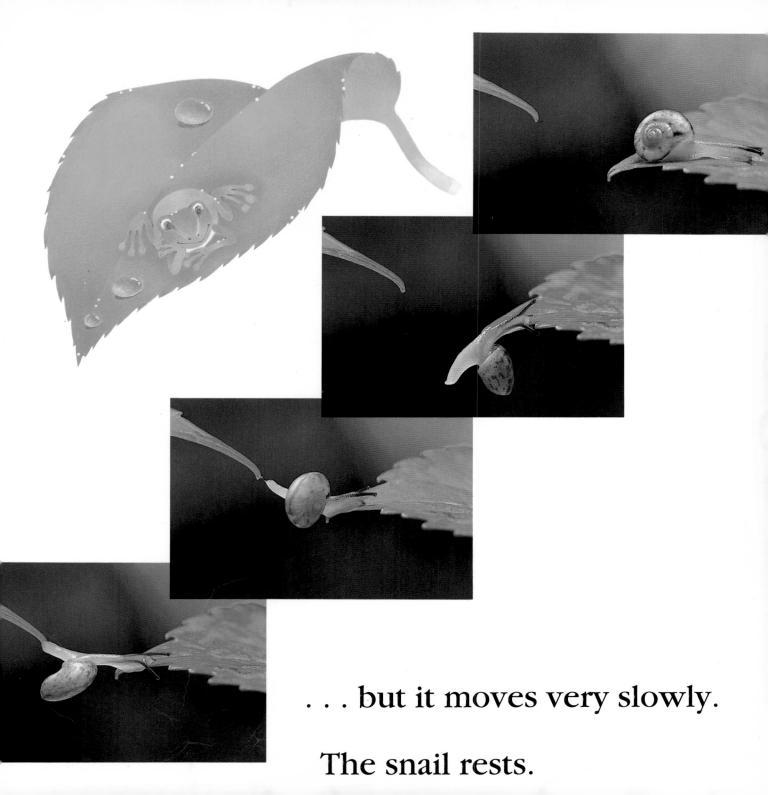

. . . but it moves very slowly.

The snail rests.

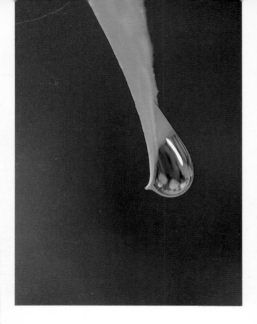

Plop, plish!

Big waterdrops land

on the little snail.

Quickly, the snail pulls in its eyes.

The rain has stopped.

The little snail crawls

to the top of the flower.

It eats bits of petal.

Such a wide world!

Where else can the

little snail explore?

Edited by Eril Hughes
Text (c) 1996 by Garrett Educational Corporation
First Published in the United States in 1996 by Garrett Educational Corporation,
130 East 13th Street, Ada, Oklahoma 74820
Copyright 1987 Kaisei-Sha Publishing Co.
Manufactured in the United States of America

Hartley, Linda
Little snail/Linda Hartley; photographs by Hidekazu Kubo
p. cm. - - (Shining nature
Photographs originally published in: Chibikko katatsumuri/Kubo Hidekaz
shashin.Tokyo: Kaiseisha, 1987, in series: Shizen kira kira
Summary: Photographs and brief text depict a snail crawling from wate
onto a leaf and encountering rain, butterflies, and a tree frog
ISBN 1-56074-067-
1. Snails- -Juvenile literature. [1. Snails.] I. Kubo, Hidekazu, ill. II. Kubo
Hidekazu.Chibikko katatsumur
Selections. III. Title. IV. Series: Hartley, Linda. Shining nature
QL430.4.H35 199
594'.3- -dc20   96-27088   CIP   A0